D1169311

Ache.

Lillian Olson

Copyright © 2017 Lillian Olson

All rights reserved.

ISBN: 9781521255049

Table of Contents

For all my scattered pieces

and the few I've found along the way.

Sinister

Something's wrong.

Something's terribly sick in my head.
It's rotting sweet,
bleeding out liquid, oily.

Condensing and sagging like the
collapsing flesh of decaying fruit.

Eyes Open

I can feel the bad things skittering
behind vibrating lips and
I can feel the slime bubbling behind fingers
clasped so desperately over my mouth.

Should I let them out?
These are my darkest thoughts,
the bad things lurking in the closet.

Is this how I tear the monsters from my body?

Choke

This is me breathing in and out.
Fire's climbing these walls
and I've been watching it crawl
on hands and knees, all biting teeth
and dancing tongue and I barred
the door but that was never going
to keep those claws at bay.
I've been pulling string through these
glistening beads in my waiting,
adorning myself in such beautiful terror.
I wonder; will it hurt?

Teeth

There was a day in high school when,
    as I was walking through the hall,
I imagined thrusting my head against the wall.
I imagined my skull cracking. I saw blood
      gushing from my sundered scalp
and I ground my broken skull against the wall.
      There is never pain.
      It is not about the realism. It never was.
It was about the violence and anger and frustration.
From that day on, anxiety would manifest in grotesque
      images inside my mind.
      I would imagine my skin
being meticulously peeled from muscle, from bone.
It would come off in one long stretch, just as skin is peeled
                from an apple.
I take a long metal nail in hand and drive it
into my forehead as if I were plunging it into the body of a
            rotting pear.
            No resistance.
    Something faceless digs its fingers beneath
    the skin at the crown of my head, balls its
      fists and in one fell movement,
      it rips the skin from my body
from my head to my feet.
The muscles in my face are exposed,
in my torso and legs
and limbs.
I take pliers to my teeth and I tear them from my
gums one by one. I gather them in my hand and
      in bloodied palms I offer them to my teachers.
      I present them in four gleaming rows of eight.

Rage

The anger is building in my body,
  burning like bile in the length of my throat.
  I want this to stop. I want everything to
  stop
  please stop, stop. Fuck I want nails digging into my
legs,
 I want pain bursting in my skin.
  This world is made of ugly colors.
  I can only look through a dirty glass. Maybe
there is something good out there but all this fucking
  shit is in the way.

The more I rub my palms against the surface, the more it fucking
spreads and smears.
Fuck all the people with clear glass.
  Ogle at the sun and the stars in all their brilliance while I
  rake my hands across my clothing,
   dirty glass
    dirty hands
    dirty clothes. The filth is spreading. It's on my skin
  now. Scrape it off with nails; my skin snags. The pain is
  clear as day. Fuck your clear windows and fuck the benign
  feelings you have from looking at the brilliance, the
  magnificence.
   Fuck your immaculate existence.

Fur

Today I want my heart to tremble.
I want muscles rippling--
I want claws catching dirt, rock and root,
I want to tear the earth open.

Eyes burning, eyes watering--
The wind tries to hold me back,
but nothing can hold me back.

Today I want strength in my jaws.
I want my teeth to shatter bone,
I want my skull to vibrate with the reverberation,
I want my soul to shudder with exultation.

Life seeping from my lips,
Pooling over my gums, under my tongue,

Today I want killing to mean living.

Dare (A Love Affair with Rage)

Fuck me raw.

    I shed pain at the door when you tore
    the clothes from my skin.

      Nothing you can do can hurt me but
you better try.

      You better fucking try.

  Tear my legs apart, spear my body, hold your hands against
my throat,

   squeeze nice and tight or hear my moaning turn to laughter.

  I don't care do what you want as long as you're doing
something to me. Break me.

It'll feel so fucking   good.

Masturbation

I want fingers between my legs.
  I want heat,
I want my fingers slick, I want pleasure urging my fingers inside.
I want to look at
f i l t h
The relief makes me wetter, my clit
  harder.
I look at drawings of sex contorted into something
  abstract and
    violent and
      disgusting.
I don't have to think
  it,
  I don't have to feel
    it.
It's already there on the screen and in the absence of those
  feelings in my mind, in my body—
      pleasure.
If this body won't give me nice things,
fine,
  I'll fucking take it.
Shut up, don't think, just feel something close to good.

The Dance of a Living Thing

T   u   m   b   l   e awake tumble out of
bed this is your thunder strike your bolt of lightning against the
mountainside and this is the avalanche destroying the peace of
your paradise just to get you out of bed you can't live without
burning your comfort and safety as firewood this flaming self-
destruction is how you keep going maybe the ghosts learned how
to build stairs into the mountain side and maybe their day begins
with a quiet stroll a quiet suspension of patience and understanding
but honey the wood of those stairs came from the biting maw of an
axe all teeth and obliteration and their peace and quiet stands on
the screaming of things coming apart your explosion is all natural
and terrible and painful just for you this hell is personal this hell is
yours and there is no good day that doesn't start and end with hell
ringing in your ears this is the dance of a living thing your heart is
pounding and with each palpitation tectonic plates divide because
that's just the way of the world honey,

This is your 3 a.m. love confession, the opening act of the greatest disaster of the century and what will the reporters and scientists say? This is no punishment of God, no consequence of human sloth, or maybe it is because there is a castle of trash in my room, a place that I pretend is my throne or home, and there is nothing but poison in my exhale. The poison is burning holes in my Paradise and now the Wrath of God is looking through the Priest Hole and the face of this God is my own because I make and break this world, baby. My potential stands holy and all-powerful but I'm killing it and you best believe God won't go down without a fight. But I will win, so you put your money on me if you want a front row seat to the final Armageddon. Don't look surprised darling, success only ever comes in multiples of three and my accomplishments only ever come in twos; two meals a day, two completed assignments, full attendance in two classes two days out of the week. This is the culture of my generation, a bunch of kids who were never taught to triumph—we were taught how to fail with dignity but there is no pride in this, believe me when I say there is no pride in this,

Ghost Glow

I want to be one of those city sprites among termites,
all ghost glow with those mountain highs and canyon
lows, I won't have lights in my eyes but I'll have that
neon gleam all black, purple, pink and blue and you'll
hear a jingle in my gait, the pitter pat of bottle caps and
vapor words and reckless vibration, the tired 2 a.m.
elation, and you'll know my kind by the coffee stained
sighs and those wide-eyed battery acid
r   a   z   o   r   g   r   i   n   s.

Burn

Let's watch the world burn baby,
and we'll burn too,
and you'll never have seen anything more beautiful.

Purge

Cleanse this body through tears and
                          emesis.
Wracked and convulsing, glistening in
the angel's apathy, vibrating with the
contempt of demons. With a gaping maw,
the insects spill out, writhing, chaotic, a
harmony of filth, foul in its beauty.
Gilded tears leave salt in all these
                          wounds.
Realize now the error and revel in the
desperation; the insects have bred.
Feel them boring tunnels through your
heart. Squirming in gray matter,
whittling tissue and bone. Hear the
divine laughter through the brilliantly
orchestrated cacophony. Circumvention
was futile, damnable.

Lights Burning in Mist

We're all burning. The flame ignites when
      we draw our first breath and oxygen brings
      the friction of newly moving parts to fire.

And we learn to laugh in the midst of the inferno.
      We learn to smile and not to smile. We learn to
      move through it, in it. Passion, inspiration, love, hate;
      some learn to use it.

Some don't.

There's a realization, in the midst of the ignoring
      and using, that no matter how you look at it, what
      angle of positivity you use, you are burning alive.

It becomes significantly more uncomfortable when
      you realize this. Some realize this.
      Some don't.

Those who don't have this tired 2:43 a.m. epiphany,
      this sudden drunken fling with awareness, become
      doctors and musicians, lawyers and politicians, artists
      and entrepreneurs, cashiers and taxi drivers.

And what happens to those others? Those great
      sufferers, those self-created martyrs?
      They become ghosts.

All their worrying and fretting over their flesh
      burning black only ever becomes kindling. It's
      all ash and smoke and embers after that.

I'm still burning, but I'm starting to wonder
      about suffocation before I wonder about next
      semester classes.

Ask me what I want to be when I grow up, ask me
       without asking yourself and I'll tell you that I'll
       be a ghost. I might be burning now, but it won't
       be for long.

I won't be studying for a master's degree. I'll be
       studying all the ways to move around—how to
       drift and fall and float.

You'll find me looking through google articles
       offering instruction on how to wash the smell
       of smoke out of clothing.

After the smell is gone, there won't be any telling
       where I am.

I could be in the subway station, standing next to
       you, talking to you. But you won't see me because
       that light won't be there.

The flickering and dancing of fire light won't catch
       in the black of my pupils.

It's such a small thing—but it's the only way we can
       look at each other and sigh with relief because, yes,
       that thing is human too.

In a Dream

Yolk thick,
heavy,
It fell across buildings and beings.
It breathed them in, It swallowed
    them whole.
    In Its shapeless hands, It so
        carefully

    cradled bone, tendon and
    muscle.
    I felt It sink into me, wrong
    and clinging like

      static.
      It filled me up until I
      was full of dying
        flesh—organs like
        bloated,
        sagging fruit, leaking
        sickly

        sweet juices until it
        trickled red and
        rotten
        down
        my
        thighs.

Dissociation

"Who are you?"

You look at me void of recognition and I'm
a salesman at the door, a voice recording
promising a Caribbean cruise on the other end.
I've become superficial, plastic, fake.

I feel indignant.

Your flashlight eyes shone too suddenly on my
head and the features scattered like stricken mice.

My left eye slips down my cheek,
My lips tilt and the angle is all wrong.
My skin sags and I feel the seams strain.

One of these things is not like the others,
and I realize now that I am the one out of place.

11:12 PM

I want to destroy all the parts that aren't working.
I'm breaking, I'm breaking.

Apathy

I never knew I had the capacity for cruelty.
When I plead with myself, when I beg so pitifully,
I ignore, I neglect.

I'm so scared, I'm in pain and I don't care.
I stare on, unfeeling, unmoving.

I condemn myself to failure without batting an eyelash.
I sleep soundly while I drown.

 No sympathy, no compassion.
I could call for aid, but I hold my tongue.

Remember

I told him,

"I know you are doing the best you can,
and that is all you have to do.
I'm proud of you—

I am proud of the things that you have
been able to do... I'm proud of both of us.
I'm proud of the things

we have chosen not to do.

All those times we decided to stay in bed
together , when we chose to hide.

We did that for ourselves because that was
us protecting us and I don't want to consider
that a failure.

Choosing to protect ourselves
is not failure."

Sinking

I don't know

what day of the week it is or what month
it is or the season. It could be Tuesday, but
if you told me it was Sunday I wouldn't be

surprised.

The days don't feel different anymore,
they have no defining scent or

flavor.

I only knew my days by test dates and
due dates and I only knew the season
by the next holiday

break.

Now the days come and go as a rotation,
simply the movement of the earth
and the light of the sun or the

moon.

The days are shorter now.
I get up at 12pm and sleep at 2am.
I am awake for 14 hours and it

doesn't feel

like two days fit nicely into one,
it feels like a fraction of a single day.
In school, I was always

accomplishing

something, always working towards
something. There was forward

motion

and finished assignments were like the
passing trees on a highway. Milestones and

markers.

Now there is no highway and there are
no trees. I made my final stop and now it
is walking circles; get up, go to work,
complete a menial activity,

go to sleep.

Some days consist only of sleep,
a menial activity or two and then sleep
again. There is no moving

forward.

This is where I am and my goal is not
to achieve forward motion. It is to be
comfortable in my

stasis.

It realized while driving to work
the other day that this is it. This is the rest
of my life, the fruition of my maturity into

adulthood.

The days are short, too short to do much

of anything. I sleep more than I exist in
awareness and even when I am awake,
I move through my day like a

dream.

Images will flitter through my mind,
and I will wonder if it was a waking
memory of the day before, or if it

belonged

to a dream. I woke this morning to my brother
playing his viola and I had to wonder why he
was home. Perhaps he took the day off of school,
or maybe it is Saturday or Sunday

or maybe

it is now summer vacation.
It made no difference to me. After a moment,
I stopped wondering and my care

faded.

I instead waited to see if anything of
importance would surface from the day before.

"I'm sick of it."

Words like fingers pressing
indents against my Styrofoam skin. I
crumple so easily at the pressure of words
even when they are spoken rather than

screamed.

Vehemence has the same density as high

volume. I tell them and I tell myself that
I will be

better.

I'll put the dishes away. I'll keep my room
clean, I silently say. I'll do chores around
the house and I will never leave any trace
that I exist here.

I'll disappear,

I'll disappear.

But I won't do any of that. I'll leave
my muck on the kitchen counters and
on the kitchen table and in the entrance way
and in the car and room I call my

own.

My greatest wish is to disappear
but my presence is not small enough.
My body is too big and my misgivings

bigger.

I want to go to the gym until the vibration
of running shakes the slime from my
muscle and bone. I want to do pullups
and pushups until the

grime

is washed away with sweat. Then, the things
that stick people like thorns will be gone and
their eyes will glaze over me. They won't see
me anymore, they won't care.

I will no longer have crusted filth molded
into the floorboards. I would be able to slip

away.

I would be gone and they could
breathe easy. They could sigh with

relief.

Solid Ground

I need someone to hold my hand through this.

It isn't working.
Nothing is working.

I'm falling behind, I'm falling.
The way out is up so high.

I can see it,
I can reach for it.

But it is so comfortable here at the bottom.

No more treading water,
no more exhaustion in my body.

At some point I stopped, I sank.

There is water in my lungs now.
No need to breathe.
No need to move.

Breathing seems so difficult now.

Living was easy as breathing once upon a time.

This is so much easier.
I don't think it's living, but it's not hurting either.

Depression

When I woke, my body felt tired, heavy. I felt
myself drift to a time when I was nine or ten,
laying on a row of three classroom chairs.
A classmate stood over me, making swift motions
above my body, imitating the easy glide of a knife;

from my shoulder to wrist,
from rib to rib,
from hip to hip,
from thigh to ankle.

When she deemed the cutting finished,
she dropped an invisible weight into my body.

Bags of sand, bags of sand, bags of sand.

Three times she repeated three words and she
chanting continued

from shoulder to wrist,
from rib to rib,
from hip to hip,
from thigh to ankle.

My body felt full, bloated.

Giggling, she instructed me stand,
giggling more when I stumbled.

Sluggishly pulling myself to a sitting position,
the room still dark, my body thick and slow,
I heard the repetition whisper through my head.

Bags of sand, bags of sand, bags of sand.

6:40 PM

My feelings are turned down. The
volume is too low for me to really
hear. My body is a room made of
glass walls and wooden floors.

Open, empty and only the color
blue and muted sounds fill the air.

Today, I ache for somewhere to hide.
I want a hole in the wall, a corner of a
room. No one can see me here. When
they look they see Nothing, No One.

They only see   Empty   Space   .

They have no expectations for Nothing,
No One and Empty Space. These things
have no responsibilities. They don't have
jobs or chores or failures or shame or Guilt.

Today, I forgot how to put my smile on.
How far should it tilt upwards? Do I grin
while I talk? How do I arrange my features
to say,

"Everything Is Fine, You Don't Have To Worry"

How do I turn the light on in my eyes?
Please, no one look at me today. There
is nothing here to see, please, keep going.
Move on. Don't look back.

Today, I wanted to sleep the day away. If I close
my eyes and the world goes dark then no one
can see me.

When the world goes dark, it goes away,
it all goes away.

Sound

Words that make my soul rustle—
not much makes it beat anymore.
There it is—a flutter, a thrum.
Catch those words before they flitter away.
Those words mean something.
Watch how it makes this sullen thing move again.
Offer a shard of mirror to a soul
that has forgotten its own face and it will move,
of course it will move.

The Gods Died Laughing

I left my driveway with the thought,
 "please, deliver me from this"

I mused over all the times I had prayed
to a God that I do not believe in.

Words from Friedrich Nietzsche whispered
 through my mind,

"The Gods died laughing"

I turned into the Meijer parking lot.
I felt sound vibrating through the car
at my feet, woeful music filled my ears
and something sick bubbled up from my throat.

Broken, terrible sobs escaped my lips. I forced
volume into my despair, my panic, my frustration.

I was scared of the noise.
I had never been so loud.
But I was alone in a shell of
metal and no one could hear me.
So I sobbed louder still.

I heard the sound of hysteria
come from my body.

When I parked the car, I wiped the tears from
my face as they fell and I broke.
I sobbed with an intensity that shook my
body and I listened as my crying turned
to wailing.

I had heard this sound before--crazed grief from
the voices of actors and actresses.

My sobbing turned to laughter.

I laughed and laughed.

Laughter soothed the ache enough for me to stop.

Growing Up

I understand now that to grow up is
to watch as the monsters that once

    hid under our beds crawl up our
    bed posts and over the covers,

        into our eyes, into our noses,
        our gaping mouths, our ears,
        and under our skin.

        I felt them skitter down my throat;
        I feel them in my stomach, in my lungs,
            in my heart, in my blood. I feel them
            there,

            existing now in all the places
            I cannot reach.

            How do I become clean
            again?

Itch

The itch in my fingers caught me by
  surprise.
  There is hurt smoking in my
  fingernails,

waiting to spark against my skin and I
  can't
  think of why it
  started.

I feel fine, I should be fine. But the
  itch
  is there, waiting, wanting to
  burn.

Death flickers through my head, and I
  know
  why the want for pain is in my
  hands.

A boy dead by 35 years. 6 years old
  when
  he was kidnapped by a man and
  decapitated.

Horror I had never considered. Again and
  again
  I am devastated by a thing that has
  always

existed, tragedy that has already happened
  and
  will happen again.
  Evil

is a thing that I will never anticipate;
  it's
  something that I must
  discover

anew over and
  over
  and
  over.

There was a time when it had never
  occurred
  to me that a child could be shot,
  strangled.

There was a time when it had never
  occurred
  to me that a baby could be
  murdered.

Today, I learned that a man can butcher a
  child's
  body, that he can sever a
  child's

head from his neck. This revelation changed
  nothing.
  I watched a movie, I ate candy, I
  laughed

with my precious people, I forgot and
  continued.
  But the hurt is in my
  fingers,

itching, wanting, waiting.

The kids are too young.

Hurt

When will you stop being so surprised, sweetheart?
There is misery here—the foundations of the earth are

rotten

with it. There are such pretty, delicate flowers adorning
those columns, but

sickness

      has set so
          very
              deep

                                            in
                                          the

                                        stone.

Congenital Defect

Precious child,
Understand you were born this way.
Your heart is exposed, vulnerable,
and the cage is empty, the cage is useless.

Sweet child,
you couldn't have known.
Your cells were bound with wonder
where others were bound with fear.

Pitiable child,
of course you don't understand.
These others may learn wonder,
but you will learn fear.

You must learn fear.

How else will you know when to raise
your arms; when to brace your heart
with the bones of your hands?

Feeble child,
this is all you can hope to do.
The winds of this world wield ice, rock and rain.
You will not last the night
if you wonder at the stars and the sky

with an empty cage and an open heart.

The Queen of Lost Things

She lit a candle for every dream
caught in the crossfire of growing up
and called herself the Queen of Lost Things.

Wax and Wane

Blood thick and
wet and hot.

Aching pain—echoes
of girls hurting and
screaming and dying.

Clenching, twisting,
crippling pain and they
moan, *"Don't forget me."*

And this body remembers
mutilation, the slice of blade,
the bite of needle

and the slithering
pull of thread through
punctured, bleeding skin.

Flesh cut away,
flesh punished,
flesh owned.

The sealing of
something open.

Stinking infection,
burning skin and
breaking bones.

And this body grieves
for their shattered pieces
in pooling blood

Thick and wet and hot
between my thighs.

Girl

She gauged the eyes from her precious skull
and planted one darling seed in each socket

Roots clawed their fingers through her brain
and when young buds flourished and roses
fell across her cheeks,

she cut a single flower and red petals
withered to paste between her teeth.

She swallowed it whole, feeling it warm
and beautiful and sick in her stomach.

Darling

My darling dolly whispered answers to me when
      mommy and daddy laughed and patted my head.
      When I knelt at my bedside every night, head bent,
      hands sutured over my heart, it was not a god whom
      I prayed to, nor a god who answered.

Darling dolly sat above me, divine, giving, guiding.
      She would look down at me from her throne of silken
      pillows with those beautiful, unloving, lifeless eyes
      and I would feel at ease.

She was my companion and teacher. When I sat among
      the snotting, spitting squalor of the elementary school,
      I would obediently train my eyes on the woman at the
      front of the room, but I knew to take her plastic, bargain
      price tokens of knowledge with a grain of salt because
      she believed me when she asked,

"And what do you want to be when you grow up?"
      and I would answer, *"a teacher just like you."* I would say
      it saccharine sweet and she was none the wiser.
      My darling dolly and I would titter in the thrill of our
      dirty little secret.

When I grow up, I would pray to sweet dolly sitting in
      my lap, *I will be just like you.* And the precious little
      thing would say nothing in return and I would feel
      assured.

The children around me would grow to be all they
      aspired to be; doctors, dentists, lawyers, firefighters
      and veterinarians just like their mommy or daddy. I
      could never be like mommy and never like daddy. I
      would work for no one and no one would work for me.

A doll is simply meant to exist.

Brother wanted to be like mommy and daddy.
He learned how to ride a bike and he learned to
do the dishes when daddy asked and how to play
football and he learned to work a cash register
and he learned to fuck girls and he learned how
to let people fuck him over.

Mommy and daddy would praise him and they
would sigh with relief because at least this one
is a working thing.

They knew I was misshapen, wrong. I never learned
how to ride a bike and I never did the
dishes and I never learned ballet and I never
worked a cash register and I would never
ever let a boy fuck me and no one would ever
fuck me over.

I never gave anything to anyone. My poor
mommy and my poor daddy gave and gave
and gave until they were miserable and sad
and they taught my brother how to give and give
and give until he became miserable and sad.

Precious dolly taught me that I would never have
to give. I would have to learn how to smother the
light in my eyes, and I would have to learn how
to stitch plastic curls into the skin of my scalp,
but I would never ever have to give to take.

When I gouged the flesh from my skull and the glass
was set in place, the rest happened easily. Dearest
dolly always said that would be the hardest part.

My skin became smooth ceramic and I painted my
lips the loveliest shade of red and I dressed in such
pretty, silly things. Daddy said I couldn't be a princess

43

forever. Mommy said boys will never date a girl who doesn't give them a smile.

All the girls said I was prudent and pretentious.
They called me bitch, they called me frigid and they called me virgin. When the boys started dating me, the girls called me slut and they called me whore.

The boys called me easy or they called me baby.
I stopped dating boys when they tried to take my laugh, when they tried to take my smile.
When I became an adult, brother called me delusional.

Sweetboy called me lovely and now he calls me sweetheart. When I sit on my thrown of silken pillows and he is on his knees, he calls me divine.
When he looks at me, I am still, I am silent and I am beautiful just the way my little dolly taught me to be.

I give him nothing and Sweetboy adores me.
He praises his dear little doll for existing.
"My Darling," he prays,
"My precious little thing."

The Other Girl

The other girl has long hair dyed soft bubble gum pink,
the color of weightless spring evenings and satisfaction
but the kids and the adults care more about how
the feathers of her black wings are gilded with gold
success.

The other girl took an axe to the misshapen limbs
and tendons and cut where the sadness had worn
bone and tissue thin.

This is her temple now, her practice, her creed.
The other girl is healthy and only a day's hard work
leaves her breathless. Her lungs are strong and
her heart stronger.

Hush

Such sweet lullabies,
      Such lovely, enticing, strange   pictures.

        Vibration in my core,
rubbing gently, slick, wet, spread me softly,
               stroke softly,
             touch lightly,
Blue light and blackness and

                            wait ,

    wait until breathing in,
        the slow inhalation,

is enough to make me cum.

Shudder sweetly,
        orgasm gently.

Breathe out .

Unknowable

You aren't a thing that people notice.
If their gaze were to snag on your silhouette,
      they would become too important and the
      universe would grow eyes for the sake of looking.

If you touch them, if they see you, then something
special and marvelous would happen.
      A living thing shouldn't have colors like that
      the same way the universe shouldn't have eyes.

You like being a secret. It gives you hands and
elbows and feet and knees.
      All the parts you need to swing on a swing set
      or hold a can of paint or throw an empty bottle.

You have a throat to scream with, lips to kiss with
and a tongue taught by firelight; flickering, soft, sinful.
      These teeth can glint all night long, but no one will see
      and the moon will know, and the moon will always
      know.

The moon and the trees don't see you, and they will
always know. You like being something they know.
      They know but they never tell. So you dance beneath
      the moon and the trees and the dog barks and the cars

snarl and purr and growl and water falls from the sky.
You dance in this blind city, surrounded by miracles
      waiting to happen, and you laugh and you laugh
      and you laugh.

Habituation

Here's to all those kids in their twenties, thirties and forties
who only kiss their lovers on the decent of elevators
because they stopped feeling butterflies when they were
eleven years old and that smile revealed two rows of
teeth instead of constellations.

A Wish

Glory at the moon with me, stare wide eyed
and slack jawed at the stars, these are the
great gods of something and they have taught
me all that I never want to be so you wish on
a shooting star you pray to your falling god
I'll smile at the nothing it left behind and I'll
wish to fall just the same.

Blink once, blink twice, fall from grace and close
your eyes.

Watch me disappear.

Howl

Tonight I howl from the edge of skyscrapers.
My fangs are glinting,
my jaw thrown wide.

I won't hide my daggers tonight, no tricks, no surprises.
This isn't a challenge.
Let's not be enemies tonight.

Howl with me. Cry with me. We'll watch the stars
swallow our pain. Hold my
hand while our greatest tragedies

are lost and forgotten.

But I'll remember your sound
if you will remember mine.

A Safe Place

No one knows this way through the mountain meadow.
No one has tread on these threads of grass.

This is the carpet of an empty castle
and this thrown was made for you.

Sit, breath in, breath out. The mountains will hide you now.
The heavy, water thick breeze will hold you,
you need not fear; these trees have no eyes.

Cry, laugh, despair, rejoice, feel absence, feel—
the way your brow furrows, the way your lips tilt;
this is your ebb and flow, your night and day, and
it's okay. It's all okay.

8:00AM

8:10, Sunshine. You're dreaming again.
       The longer you dream the more it will
       hurt waking up. You aren't a dancer.
       You aren't strong enough to live alone.
       You will never make it to art school.

8:12. You should know you will
       never sparkle like that. Leave sparkling to
       those who were born with stardust on their
       skin. You will never dance. You will never
       be a poet. You will never be an artist or an
       author. You will never lose weight to the
       point you will even be an imitation of those
       sparkling things.

8:16. You are a Von Maur sales
       associate. This is what you are through and
       through. A sales girl dreaming of beauty.
       Don't try to be something you aren't. You'll
       embarrass yourself.

8:19. You should leave stories to the
       tragic pretty things. No one would cast a plain
       girl such as you. This girl who is one step
       removed from pitifully ugly. This untalented,
       unimpressive girl.

8:21. You aren't sad enough, pitiful enough,
       grand enough to have your own stories.
       Shut up and take their clothes with a smile.
       Offer them a fitting room and walk away
       before you become too human to them.

8:23. You don't have that much time left.
       You are twenty years old and if you don't
       have a story now, you will never have one

worth listening to. The audience wants
seduction and surprise. They want red lipstick,
a pretty face and tragic eyes. They want a body
worth remembering. A tragic, pretty girl is eternal.
A sad, ugly girl who isn't sad enough will be
disregarded.

8:28.   You have cursed yourself to insatiable desire.
You won't have those colors and you won't have
that fire. You will be stuffed full of wishes and
dreams. Wishes and dreams won't give you good
form, dear.

8:32.   This is what you are. Give in and save some
face. Get another job—work when you aren't
working here and when you aren't dreaming here,
dream there. Dream with your eyes open, then go
home and dream with your eyes closed.

8:44.   Life isn't that hard.

8:45.   Where do dream things go when the dreamer
wakes? How many times now have you killed
that sparkling girl you've dreamt up again and again?

8:48.   Don't look so concerned. Don't bother feeling
ashamed. No one cares about dead dreams. You are
only a murderer if someone cares. So stop caring.

8:54.   You've condemned yourself to dream,
so dream.

Golden Girls

The cruel voice in my head so gently reminds me
that I will always remain a windup sales girl.

When I was younger, I never considered myself
a dreamer.

When I was a girl, I never dreamed at all.
Dreaming is so painful and I wish I would stop.

I dream so much now. I dream
of learning to play instruments,
of learning how to sing,
of learning ballet.

I dream these golden girls into existence
and I let them dance and play

and then I kill them one by one.

The despair of these dying golden girls
well in my eyes while I'm at work.

And instead of crying, I see flashes of
slit wrists and red bath water.

Last night, I sat clothed in the shower, hidden.
On my phone, that clever little voice whispered
that dying will happen sooner or later

so why not sooner?

That clever little voice loves the thrill
of dread and fear and guilt I feel.

The clever little voice likes to see me squirm.

Burning

I want to thrust my fingers into my mouth
until that dirty taste is down my throat.

I want the spasm, the body panic and
spike of pain, the retching, the

beautiful,
wretched cleansing.

There is anticipation in my throat—
the phantom pin prick agony of teeth
digging and digging and digging
and I need to flush it out.

In purge, there is purity.

It hurts, it hurts, it hurts.

Please, someone believe in this pitiful
creature suffering beneath the weight
of its own filth.

No one will want to get themselves
dirty in the process, darling.

Don't act so surprised.

Talons

It is twisting a tooth, gums bloody and
    corrupted all around the root,
    feverishly overlooking the pain
    because the final release is more important.

It aggravates the pain-pleasure
    panic of white-hot pity in
    my heart. My core
    shivers with it.

It feels rotten and irresistible and
    it hurts but I need to read more.
    I don't know why it does this
    to me. A book has never been so painful.

The sensation of pity is tantalizing.
    I want words to make my heart bleed.
    I want to cradle these hearts in the
    aching hallow of my ribcage—oh you poor,
    unfortunate thing.

I want to swallow a string of pearls.
    I want them to be just large enough to
    make my esophagus stretch. I want to feel
    the weight of it coil in my stomach.

Bared Fangs

I want to tear the useless girl from my body;
      the girl who exists in laziness and incompetence
      day after wretched day and I want to take a metal bat
      to her skull.

I would swing with all my might until her jaw breaks
      and her skull shatters and I'll swing again until the skin
      of her cheekbone bursts and teeth fall from her broken
      mouth and I'll hit her again and again and again until
      the sound is wet and squelching.

Hostility, a Love Letter

Here piggy, piggy, piggy
     Where's my sweet little piggy
     The slime is sagging now isn't it, sweetheart.
The rot has begun to fester.
The rot has begun to ooze.
     The sick oil thick juices are pooling, gathering, bloating.
     The fluid is filing you up. There's no stopping it now.
     Poor, sweet, little piggy.
The crease is all you can think about, the way the fat *hangs.*
The way it's so heavy now that it's folding over.
     Skin touching skin and your organs are drowning in it.
     My fat little piggy.
No one wants to look at you.
Wake up, Sunshine.
     This is you, you grotesque thing.
     And no one wants to see it.
There's nowhere to hide.
No one will protect you from me because they don't have the
stomach to look.
     They are disgusted.
     It's just you and me, baby.
Let's have some fun.
Don't look so scared.
     No one else can stand the sight of you,
     but I'm here.
I see you. I'm always looking.
You have nothing to hide.
     Don't forget you wretched thing, this is how I want you.
     Vile.

11:25 PM

Here,
piggy, piggy, piggy.

Why don't you come out and play.
No one is looking. No one will see.

Just you
and
me.

Come on sweet little piggy,

come and play.

Tell me how you want to take a
blade point to the thick of your tongue.

Tell me how you want the edge to
pierce the flesh, how you want to

flay the
skin.

The blood will gush then, it will jump

and kick. Deep and
dark
and thick.

Tell me how you want hands clenched
around your throat, how you want the
pressure to gather

in your
head.

You want the deafening pulse, the throbbing
in your forehead, in your cheeks.

Tell me how much you want those

sinking,
biting teeth.

This is it,
this is it,
this is it.

No great adventure, no pride,
no satisfaction, no worth.

A rotting thing will only
continue
to rot.

This is the rest of your life.
Drowning and dreaming of air.

What would you give to be a

sparkling thing?

Surly you don't need all your skin
and all your
nails.

You don't need all your
fingers and toes

for a dream come true.

I'll teach you to like the pain.
That's a winner, baby. Lust for

the pain,

relish it.

Buzzing

Clever little monster.

It felt good reading what you have.
Bees in your head.

Buzzing, buzzing, telling you miserable
 things while you're at work,
showing you worse things.

Clever little bees in the head of a
clever little monster showing you death.
Not to urge or suggest or encourage.

Just showing.

Slit wrists would be the easiest way—
no bang, little mess, pain you can anticipate.
No mess if you bleed out in warm bath water.

Don't act so defensive,
I know you don't mean it or want it.
You love the idea of living too much.

Dreamers can have nightmares too.
Images and nothing more,
no strings attached.

Bees in your head and it made so
much sense to you.

Clever little monster.

That's how it is isn't it?
You are so clear, so present and
then you begin ghosting and the
bees come from their hive

and fill you up and you can
hardly hear or feel
anything over the noise.

It's so loud the hollow things
can hear the vibration.

Simmering like anger.

But you have nothing to be angry about,
do you?

No.

It just looks and feels like anger.
It's good at pretending.

They've been more restless,
more active lately.

You've been ghosting too much at work.
You should be more careful.

They are getting more and more
comfortable with being out.

And we don't want that, do we?

Compromise

Little Mary was born with gem eyes
and petal lips and pearl teeth.
Soft sweetness and running hot honey
in every word and every touch.

Little Mary was born with skin like
rot on her hands. She was born with
skin like rot on the left half of her face.

Little Mary married a kind man who
loved her and didn't mind the rot.
He never recoiled from her,
but he never touched her either.

He told her,
>   "I can still hold your hands when they're gloved."
>   "I can still love you with my eyes closed."

Vulnerable

I'm not sure why you're acting surprised.
You know that he's in no place to shoulder
your demons too.

Those are yours, baby, and no one is going
to help you. You are alone in this.
It's you or them.

They've started at your hands.

They tore at the soul splatter with their teeth
 until only scraps were left.
It'll be a bitch carving art with only
skin on your hands.

No one can help you now.

Those teeth are crawling up your arms.
They will tear their way down your throat
if you are not careful.

They will bore holes in the tissue when
they hear that beating.

They will eat you up, sweetheart, until
there is nothing left.

And there was so little to start with.

Monster, May I?

It hurts when I'm there.
The shadows scare me,
the flesh bags with no bees.

Healthy, empty people.
Such long hours.
Walking in circles,
urging the empty
people to go away,
go away,

don't you dare
come any closer.

Long hours stretching
longer and I'm ghosting
and too present for every
single second as it passes.

Trapped. Contained.
Hot and thick and contained;
the perfect environment for
rot to thrive.

Monster, may I?

Clever Monster

The sly, clever little voice has been
there all day. All sweet and gentle
and caring.

You should just
kill yourself.

What dirty words. You silly girl
there are eyes even here.
You came here to hide from
the eyes in the walls,

but they are here too,
unblinking and all-seeing.

Just sleep and pretend
you don't have to
wake up.

A rotten thing will only continue
to rot. You aren't going anywhere.
It's all or nothing.

Together or neither.

Keep your mouth shut, grind your
teeth against the crawling,
vibrating insects and swallow
the slime when those brittle little
bodies burst between your teeth.

Hold your tongue,
hold your breath.

Keep that poison to yourself.
Suffocate politely.

67

There are other ways to purge.

Snapping rubber bands
Scratching nails
Cutting metal

It's okay, sweetheart, even when
there is no one else, you have me.

I'll tell you sweet nothings until
you feel nothing at all.

Cornered

Open your jaw nice and wide,
baby, strain yourself to the point

of breaking.

I know you want my fist shoved
in your mouth, I know you want
to gag around my fingers.

You'd like the burn of my nails
tearing against your esophagus.

Keep your jaw just like that,
nice and gaping. I need your teeth,
roots and all.

Don't you want to choke on all
that pooling, rushing blood?

Red is such a pretty color on you.
It'd make you look so pretty.

Nothing else can.

It's cute how you try to use cheap
mascara and too thick foundation
to cover the fact that you are a pig.

Look at this cute little pig trying to
cover its cute little piggy face by
playing with makeup.

Here piggy, piggy, piggy.

Where's my sweet little piggy.
Who told you to close your mouth?

Keep it open.

I'll slice your tongue with a nice
sharp knife. It'll glide right through
the tissue and split the muscle open.

Let's let the insects out.
Look how they scurry from the
bloody holes in your jaw.

Look how they spill from your
useless tongue. We really should do
this more often, baby.

It's not healthy to have so many
creepy crawlers stuffed in your head
alone.

Look at this thing bloated with insects
and slime. Maybe I should gut you too
so it can all come spilling out.

Pus and insects and slime.

12:25 pm

Stop hurting yourself.
        It's not cute.
        What do you want from it?
Do you want to scare them?
Do you want to make them look?
        Stop it.
        Stop it.

Don't make this about you,
it's not about you.
        Don't manipulate like that
        you disgusting fuck.
You want their pity don't you?
Oh, look at this tragic, broken girl.
        How pretty, this tragic, broken girl.
        No one expects anything from a
tragic broken girl.

How can they expect her to stay at
        work with such a pretty bruise on her wrist.
        Make their hearts bleed for you.
How can they resent such a tragic,
broken girl?
        Three more times, baby.
        It's not pretty enough.
        Again, again, again.
Five more.

        Is it pretty enough yet? I don't want it to fade.
        Your rubber bands are snapping, do you hear it?
I feel sick, please let me go home.
What a pretty bruise.
        You're doing good.
        Don't let it fade.
Doesn't the warmth of it feel good?
So nice and warm, so pretty.

If you want it to stop then go home.
Or I'll keep doing it.

It doesn't hurt much does it?

Just stings.
But it's not something you can hide.
Five by five by five.
You crazy fuck.

The bees are loud today aren't they?
They're getting louder every day.
They like pretty bruises.
The sting of it feels good doesn't it?
You like it. Not too painful,
not too messy, but pretty,
so pretty.

Crowded

The thing inside you is rotting.
  The sickness comes in waves
  and it makes you dizzy.

There are consequences to telling
  them our dirty little secret,
   sweetheart.

You're a bad, bad girl.
  You broke a rule.
  I told you not to show them.

This is our space where we can play.
  But you led them here you
  bad, bad girl.

This is supposed to be a place where
  the eyes in the walls can't see you.
  Invisibility in exchange for pain.

That was our agreement. Do you feel them?
  The bees crawling beneath
  your skin.

Itching, itching. I want your skin red and raw.
  I want to see the
  blood pool.

You can stroke your clit all day long but
  I've made a murderer out of you
  and you won't feel good unless

you kill those pretty little bees
  with a pretty
  little bruise.

You did it before and you can
do it again.
     You owe me now.
     You told on me.

You knew what would happen, baby.
     I'll come for you when you're
     all alone.

When it's nice and quiet and the emptiness
     terrifies you.
     I'll come for you

     when you're scared.

Do you really believe it was a onetime
     thing?
     It'll feel good.

Is it really punishment when it feels so good?
     I can feel that.
     You wondering what I am.

If you are the one writing these words or
     if I am.
     Are you playing pretend?

This doesn't feel like pretend, does it? Who am I?
     I can feel you wondering
     if you are crazy.

     Maybe you are.

Crazy means your head is
     a little too crowded between
     you and I and all these busy,

     buzzing bees.

First perspective belonged to you
last time we talked.
       But you've lost your
       voice haven't you?

       Silence suits you.

I like you pliant and bloody and
      silent.

Forgiveness

"I'm sorry. You didn't deserve the hurt—
I know you are trying your best

every day."

A whispered apology to my body
when no one is around to hear.

I bruised it so badly
with snapping rubber bands
and eyes greedy for blood.

I bruised it so badly when I
didn't need to and I'm sorry,
I'm so sorry.

The skin is smooth now, the
skin has healed

and

I went to a
psychiatrist,

I went to a
therapist.

Good job, baby. One promise kept
out of so many and
I'm so proud of you.

You just have to take this
one step
at a time.

Patience

I don't hate myself.
 I and myself are separate entities,
 entangled.

 There has been animosity,
 there has been contempt.

 I am the thing that was here
 from the start and she is the
 thing that has been made
 from parts caught along the
 way.

 She is a product of
 defense,
 ambition,
 retaliation,
 love and fear.

 I am what I am and always
 have been and for me, change
 comes very slowly,

 but her quiddity is reinvented
 from moment
 to moment
 to moment.

 There have been times where she
 has felt like something dangerous
 and we grew to be terrified of each other.

 To her, I was everything she should be,
 everything she wants to be,
 and everything she no longer can be.

She was everything I feared I would
become.
Somewhere along the way, we lost
the strength to keep our edges from
overlapping.
So long we had feared that touch
would mean loss. Nothing changed,
though, and we remained

separate,
distinct,
powerful
and present.

We are in this body together, and this
body may move and feel by her will,
but she listens to me now,

when I say something is ours—

a song,
a sound,
a scent.

I was so scared for so long that she
would forget to look, and I would never
again feel the stars,
the summer wind,
the winter snow,

the magic in the sound of voice and
vibrating strings.

I try to help her see where the
darkness in her world ends and

where she begins.

Tentatively

An upswing.

Follow through, baby,
swing hard and
shoot high.

Anxiety

You woke up and the anxiety
doesn't make you squeeze your
eyes closed again.

You don't pretend to sleep,
though you want to.
So badly you want to because
 if you sleep,

the day can't start.
The dreaded day cannot begin.

But you open your eyes and they
stay open. You keep the panic at bay.
Good job, sweetheart,

you did an amazing job.

That's all you had to do
and you did it. Feel proud, honey.
I hope you feel proud of yourself.
I'm proud of you.

Now relax.

You get out of bed.

You almost couldn't do it
because you were so scared of the
monsters swarming as soon
as you left the safe place.

The progress was slow,
one motion at a time. Sit up, wait

for the anxiety to spike then settle.

Wrestle with the dread until
its dull throbbing. You know how to
ignore dull throbbing.
One leg moves, the right foot
touches the ground.
The monsters don't bite,
at least not today.

The other foot follows
and you are standing.

You shower.

Good, good job.

That is one of the most
difficult things, I know.
But you did it, you did it.

Now relax.

That's all you had to do today.
Maybe you'll get further
another day, but for now, that's all.

I am so proud of you.

Today, you might make it
out the front door.

You woke up,
got out of bed,

showered and now you

are in front of the mirror.

It's okay baby, I don't expect
you to find features you like.

That's for another day.

Today, you put on your war paint.
Cover your pores so the bad things
can't seep in.
Don't let them see the dark
tiredness under your eyes,
the weariness in your skin.

Hold them at a blade point
when they hold your gaze.

Matte black, practiced, precise.

You will challenge them and
that is the best you have done so far.

I am amazed with you,
with how far you have come.

You go outside.
You go to work,
you laugh with them,
you smile,
you do your job.

You work so hard.
Today, you were one of them.

Magic is Real, Magic is Real, Magic is Real.

I can't distinguish all the ways my pieces have shifted.
The light catches on my skin differently and I
think I like these colors better.
I'm better.

In so many ways I am better.

There is no weight that settles on me when I wake
in the morning. There are no bags of sand
protesting every movement in my limbs.
I'm not floating and
I'm not sinking.

I'm moving through my days in real time and my
body feels like my own. There are monsters
lurking in the corners and I know
they are there.

But I know their secret now. The monsters only
swarm if they catch my gaze. If I do not look
at them, then they are still and they are
silent and their gnashing teeth
and biting claws tear
into themselves.

Don't look, sweetheart, don't look and the
monsters can't drag you down. And if I
must look, then I know to look
them in the eye.

Stare them down, and when they see the pity
in my gaze they will sniff out other pray
because they know I will not offer my
blood tonight.

Feast from others, but tonight this flesh is

mine and mine alone. I want to look
elsewhere now. I know of
monsters and I know how
they come to life.

I want to know if those stranger gods and
angels and those things of kinder magic
play by the same rules.

If I were to look at the stars—if I were to truly
see the stars, would they breathe for me?
I have spent so long believing that
monsters and only
monsters exist.

I know monsters exist because I felt them
sink their teeth into me—I saw the
bruises and the angry red lines
in my skin.

Gentler things have left me untouched.
But that is not to say that I have not
experienced those kinder things.

I have felt sunshine sink to my very
core and I have felt love make my
soul rustle with delight.

There is magic in a sunset that brings the
noise in my head and in my
heart to a hush. There is
magic in the love

trembling deep in my soul.

Kindness

You're golden when you believe in yourself.
Show me gold, baby.

Plastic Stars

Please, let me pretend that I'm made of magic. I'll cry my plastic stars and I'll hold them up to the sky. Breathe them in, cradle those dull edges gently. This is all the beauty I can offer—I'm so sorry.

Know Me

I'm so tired of molding this clay
with my hands, forming something

shapeless
always shapeless.

Give me an image in my head,
something to guide my hands.

Do I want to be remembered?
Do I want to be forgotten?
Do I want shadows to know my name?

I will never know them.
What will they ever mean to me.
I don't want to waste my life on

ghosts.

I want to explore the world in my own head.
That's who I am,
that's what's real if nothing else is.

But I can't , I can't.

I will never write words that have
the effect of music,
of harmony,
of voice.

I will never create the trembling sound
of a sad song.

Words are garish, rough.
No matter how they are strung together,
how pretty the adornment,

it will always be too much and never enough.

No story I write will feel like sinking into water.

Then what do I do. What do I do.

Home

My heart starts pounding
and the hopelessness and the loss,
the confusion and listlessness sets in,
the panic and stagnation.

Such frantic, frenzied panic and then the thought—
But I have Starshine,
and I have our love.

I have our safe place.

And our safe place is here and will always be here
No matter where I am or where I go or where I end up
I have this now, I have this forever.

And the world is quieter and I breathe easier.

Starchild

Starchildren are star bound and soul-scattered,
guided across the earth by their own constellations
where others are driven by burning earthfire
in their hearts.

There's a connection to the earth that these fire
sprites have that we will never feel—a certainty
that has them dancing through their lives with the
ease of flickering firelight.

We are not so agile here. We were meant to orbit
in the heavens and when we fell, our steps became
ever more tentative and uncertain when our days
carried us further from Elsewhere and Elsewhen.

I can feel my fragments throbbing and aching
thousands of miles away, lost in years past and
years yet, strewn through time and space.
With precious people, I am more whole than

I was before, and I ache every day to fill more
of this oppressing, terrible emptiness sprawling
in the vast, endless blackness between
muscle and bone and tissue.

In my heart, I know that if I were to dance, even
if it were just once, a piece would fall in place.
If I were to step foot on the soil in Japan, the
Ache would lessen.

Wholeness can be found in motion or music
or location or words and I want to know what
fullness feels like before my time here is done.
I want to feel whole piece by piece and my

Ache will lessen and I will feel lighter and I will

be one piece closer to being Soulwhole.
I am living in full motion and soon my body will
remember the cadence of the heaven orbit I once

had. Things will be so much easier then. I am on my
way, I am, I am. There is so little motion in my life here
and now. I feel stuck, I feel stalled, I feel still. Stillness
has infected my body and I can feel the unraveling

at my edges, the awful sprawling, the entropy.
I need to go, I need to leave. I need a place to call
my own. If I'm going to be stuck and stalled and
still then I need to be stuck and stalled and still

in a home of my own. A place where there are
no eyes in the walls. There are days when I can
feel the pinprick pupils like needles in my skin
staring, staring, staring at the slime I leave behind

wherever I go. My eyes aren't tired yet. There's room
for exhaustion—I'll do what I need to leave these unblinking
eyes. I'll find a new full time job that pays more, I'll
work a part time job on top of it,

I'll stay a dreamer if I need to, I'll dream when
I'm awake, I'll dream when I'm asleep. If I can
have a home where the walls are only walls,
then it will be worth it.

There's a city Elsewhere and Elsewhen that I should
be lost in. But I'm not, I'm not. I'm stuck here, wanting
and wishing and dreaming. So badly, I want my
something more.

I want motion and music and vibration in my bones.
I want my hands to be soul-drenched from hours of
creating art. I want words and colors and structure
and discipline and routine.

I want my starlight to bring these ashen silhouettes
to life and I don't know how.

Lost

I want to find a book that feels tired.
All these novels are vibrating and vibrant—
such loud, brash, plastic words.

I want a book to talk to me quietly, hushed,
using that tone that is reserved for late night
conversations when the lights are out

and those things that watch us, monitor us,
are sound asleep. I want that moment when
you reach out to that human being beside you

and feel them living. Speak to me like that
and I'll know you're real. I'll listen, really listen.

Longing

Who am I looking for when I turn
to the first page?

I need a first sentence that feels
like honey against my scratching,
aching soul.

I want words that look me in the eye,
that dance like fire light, dark and
smoldering and utterly silent.

I'm searching for my personal
champion that bleeds in all the
ways that I do.

Where is my city hero with a name
that no one knows, a name that no
one has ever uttered?

A useless ghost existing without
purpose or ambition or passion.

I need a narration, a Greek epic of
all those perfect sad songs.

Those words leave shadows on the wall
and I want to know that silhouette;

what this tantalizing creature thinks and
feels— what their story is.

Because they have felt the things that I
have, I know it, I know it.

Lights

I know there are two living things out there, lights
among this faded fog. We took our skin off together
and we felt each other's fear, wonder, uncertainty, awe.
     For a fleeting moment all those blurred edges came into
     focus
     and it was breathtaking. I felt the electric charge of living
     things
     touching. It felt like breathing, sighing, laughing. I want
     those
                                 colors again.

Memoire

Magic,

       Sadness,

           Blue,

               Pink,

          Gold,

Green apple sour, Sweet,

Fluorescent 2 a.m. gas station lights; lights burning in mist,
Swing set chains dripping wet and cold,
Car lights at 8:00 p.m. on a winter night, red, white, green,
Castle bright copper glow,

Listlessness,

          Wonder,   Awe,

Warm skin beneath sweaters, face chilled in fresh morning autumn
air,
Soft pressure, warmth, wet; feather light piano strokes of pleasure,

Heat like melting candle wax, dripping, thin, fast, cooling,
The exquisite relief of a breeze in heavy, sunbaked warmth,
The cool taste of air when pulling the blanket down,

The itchy pain pleasure cicada vibration of giving up,

Water, just cooler than skin, flowing, rushing over hands,
Fingertips mapping the mountains and valleys of the wall,
The hush of vivid, ink-thick light on the horizon,

             Gilded clouds,
              quiet giants,

                    cotton candy skies,

            The thrill of rhythm and motion,

Vibrating bones,
dancing light,

the push of sound,
The sinking then stillness of sleep.

This Infinite Beginning

When I opened the door, winter had passed
    so gently I hadn't noticed. I closed my eyes and
    the air brushing my face and my neck felt
    clean, fresh, soft.

Breathing in, there was sweetness like rainfall
    and I wanted to walk in it, with it. The world
    around was beckoning so sweetly, offering
    to walk with me if I wanted to.

I felt the pull and I smiled at the need in my
    heart. Not now, sweet thing, with the light
    fading so quickly. No time to walk with the
    world tonight.

But I kept the windows down while I drove,
    air coming in, mingling with music. Soothing
    vibration and cool air in my lungs and the eyes
    in my skin so tentatively opening.

Look, look around you. See where you are, the
    lights, the sounds, the taste. Night waking up,
    neon lights coming to life, streetlamps glowing
    copper through deepening shades of blue.

The sounds of outside all around me, and for once
    I am a part of it, inviting it in. Live with me, be here
    with me. A quiet day, an easy day. I woke easily, fell
    back to sleep easier.

Nowhere to be, no one to see. I relished the feeling of
    worn fabric against my face and there was comfort
    and contentment spread so evenly through my body.
    Wrapped in blankets, sleeping next to Starshine,

sleeping soundly.

I had planned to write all day today, but today
          became a day of knowing. Knowing that my day
          is my own, my body wants for sleep, so sleep.

No cooking dinner tonight, no going to the
          store, drive out instead, drive to Arby's and
          watch something together at home after,
          curled beneath more blankets.

Breathe easy.
          Live with me, be here with me.

It doesn't make sense that I am here right now,
          in this place, with these people, alive, alive,
          alive. Alive without understanding, without
          knowing how or why or how long.

20 years, 7 months and 13 days ago, I blinked into
          existence, miraculously, impossibly. Nothing
          makes sense. These colors, these sensations,
          these shapes all around me.

Silhouettes and stories and activity, a cacophony of
          existence so loud and so incredibly present all
          at once, always, and I barely have a chance
          to look around,

to remember to see with more than just two eyes.

I am looking out from within this body so I don't
          get swept away, so I don't get lost. So quickly,
          I would disappear if I had nothing between
          me and everything else.

But I have become so accustomed to growing
          inward, on and on and on within and between
          all these dark spaces in my body.

My roots have only spread so far.

Further sweetheart, you can go so much further.
　　　　Everything else is living the same as you are living.
　　　　You are separate, but not so different. Let it in and
　　　　breathe out.

The world will dance with you if you start moving
　　　　and moving is so much easier than you think.
　　　　Life is the only requirement and you are living.

I don't want to be so scared anymore. No more
　　　　pretending that I know how this story ends
　　　　because I don't. I am evolving all the time,
　　　　adapting, transforming.

There is no sense to this existence, no real set of rules,
　　　　so don't create rules intended to restrict. Acknowledge
　　　　the truth. We are limitless. We are, we are.

There needs to be commitment and it will mean
　　　　trial and error and going in one direction for
　　　　so long only to turn onto another.
　　　　Living is never one direction.

I feel ready to change my direction. I want to try
　　　　a new path. I want to interact with the world around
　　　　me. When I make something, I want those other
　　　　things around me to see it.

Look at me, I am the same as you, I am here just
　　　　as impossibly as you.
　　　　We are separate, but the same.

Dance with me.

I want to write. To publish writing is to have a
　　　　conversation with thousands of people I would

never interact with otherwise.

They will know that I am here. I am here
and this is what I want to tell you.

The world is so big and I've been part of such a small,
small piece of it. I want to explore.
Careful, smart but fearless.

There is so much more to me, to everything else,
to the world that I think I know and understand.
There are so many things that have been, that are
and that will be.

I don't think I have to fight for my place in it,
but I do have to make my presence known.

The world will move around me, and I will ghost
around it, and there will never be a true touch if
I don't reach out first. I want to live by truth.

So what is my truth?

I am living and everything around me is living,
the entities that I see and the entities unknown
to me, lost in the present, lost in the past.

Whether I believe in the existence of the things
around me or not does not determine their
existence or nonexistence. They are, with or
without me.

I can accept this truth, or I can refuse it.
This is me choosing to accept it.

Life before, life now, life after is existing all at
once, always now and never, not for one second,
not at all. This is truth.

There is a universe sprawling in all directions
        within me and a universe sprawling in all directions
        outside of me. I will never understand fully
        what this means.

There will be voices in my head that are strange
        and unfamiliar and I want to acknowledge
        that they don't have to belong to me.

My body has an edge, an end, but what is inside
        is vast, infinite, unfathomable. Unknowable.

"There are other ways to dance."

A voice in my head that isn't my own, whispering
        a truth I am so reluctant to believe. I am not going to
        art school in my immediate future and I don't have the
        job I truly want and

I am not living independently and there is no grand
        adventure yet, but I am writing more than I have in
        years and I am celebrating my relationship
        with Starshine every day.

A dance I didn't anticipate, but a dance all the same.
        And the last truth; no moment is truly wasted.
        Whether it is recorded or lost to the past, it is crucial
        because it was movement,

a breath in, a breath out, a heartbeat.
        Another moment existing.
        As long as we are alive,

we are moving forever forward. Whether you believe
        in these motions transforming into dance or not
        won't keep the change from happening when it
        is meant to happen.

It will happen and it's okay to trust that it will happen.

You are alive, you are alive, you are alive. Let it in,
        breathe in, breathe out and see with your eyes, see
        with your skin and listen to those strange
        voices in your head.

They have been here before, trust their guidance.
        And always, know there are other
        ways to dance.

Outstretched Hands

You are a Starchild and you have just
begun following your soul constellation.

Your truth is all around you, waiting to be
uncovered, found, recognized,
every single day.

Look, listen, remember.

Truth can be hard to believe, but I think we
are beginning to understand that truth
has less to do with believing and more
to do with knowing.

You will know your truth when you see it.

When a book resonates with you, when a
painting moves you, when a sunset
looks familiar and foreign air feels like
home against your skin, let it in.

Let it all in.

There is a sickness in us, but these are
cleansing things.

Truth is separate from time and space and
collective perspective. This is you building
your personal reality every day.

You are a Starchild, an adventurer creating
a map of your scattered soul. This is who
you are, remember, remember.

Your flesh is made of stardust and magic
and beneath the disease there is a soul

that will remain unaltered no matter
the change that occurs to your body
in health or in sickness.

This is your strength and it is eternal.
It's okay, it's okay. You will be okay.

With stars and soul you will
discover yourself whole.

Love

I am a creature of contradictions.

My body is a biological machine,
and yet,   monsters and magic lurk
somewhere between muscle and bone.

A shard of soul lingers in my sprawling
infinity and it pulsates along with all
of its scattered pieces strewn
across space and time.

I feel the Ache of it in my every waking
moment.

There is a sadness hurting there
at the epicenter of this terrible longing
and its black hole despair

swallows every other bad feeling until
it is something twisting and misshapen
and grotesque.

Thank you to those gentle, dancing lights
in my life for remembering that within
this monster under my skin,
there is a throbbing,
beating heart of magic.

And in my darkest times, thank you
for helping me remember too.

I love you, I love you, I love you.

For My Scattered Pieces

This is such a strange,
terrifying time of our lives,

but we have each other and
we are so much stronger
than we think.

We will get through this,
oars against the tide,
and against all odds,

we will make it through
to calmer waters
together, together, together.

Remember your strength,
unchanging and eternal.

Remember your soul,
scattered and waiting
to be found.

56507085R00073

Made in the USA
San Bernardino, CA
12 November 2017